CASE
FOR
CHRIST
FOR KIDS

UPDATED AND EXPANDED

NEW YORK TIMES BESTSELLING AUTHOR

LEE STROBEL

WITH ROB SUGGS AND ROBERT ELMER

CASE
FOR
CHRIST
FOR KIDS

UPDATED AND
EXPANDED

ZONDER**kidz**

ZONDERVAN.com/
AUTHOR**TRACKER**
follow your favorite authors

ZONDERKIDZ

Case for Christ for Kids, Updated and Expanded
Copyright © 2006, 2010 by Lee Strobel and Robert Elmer

Requests for information should be addressed to:
Zonderkidz, *Grand Rapids, Michigan 49530*

Library of Congress Cataloging-in-Publication Data

Strobel, Lee, 1952-
   Case for Christ for kids / Lee Strobel with Rob Suggs and Robert Elmer. —
   Updated and expanded.
     p. cm.
     ISBN 978-0-310-71990-8 (softcover)
     1. Jesus Christ — Person and offices — Juvenile literature. 2.
   Bible — Evidences, authority, etc. — Juvenile literature. I. Suggs, Rob. II. Elmer,
   Robert. III. Title.
   BT203.S77 2010
   232.9'08 — dc22   2009037506

Zonderkidz is a trademark of Zondervan.
Editor: Kathleen Kerr
Art direction: Kris Nelson
Cover design: Jody Langley
Interior design & composition: Luke Daab and Carlos Eluterio Estrada
Illustrations © 2010 by Terry Colon

Printed in the United States of America

20 21 PC/LSCH/ 30 29 28 27 26

TABLE OF CONTENTS

Introduction:
WHAT'S UP WITH THAT?

S omewhere you took a wrong turn.
This is just the kind of street Mom and Dad warned you to avoid. Run-down apartment buildings line both sides of the road and the sidewalk is cluttered with garbage. Dirty faces leer at you from the darkness.

You need to be home soon, but who can help you? One friendly face emerges from the shadows. She's a young girl — about your age. She smiles and says her name is Lydia Delgado. She tells you how to get back to your neighborhood.

You think about Lydia later, and ask your mom if you can go back to thank her. "Only if I go with you," says Mom. So you climb into the car and track down Lydia and her family. There are only two others: a thirteen-year-old sister, Jenny, and their grandmother, Perfecta. The two sisters have no parents.

What's more, they live in an empty little room with no furniture, no food, and no warmth. Lydia and Jenny take turns wearing one sweater as they walk to school. That makes you and Mom sad, but the three women who live there seem to be full of smiles.

Your mom has a friend who writes for the newspaper. She tells her the story of the Delgado family and says, "Write an article! Your readers need to know about our poor neighbors who need food and shelter."

Christmas Day arrives. You open your gifts and enjoy a scrumptious turkey dinner. But after dinner, your family decides to pay the Delgados a visit. You have gifts for them and extra turkey and vegetables. So again, you climb into the car.

And a Christmas miracle has happened!

Newspaper readers have sent the Delgados boxes and bags of Christmas gifts: warm coats and sweaters for the family, carpets and chairs for the little apartment. A magnificent Christmas tree illuminates the room, and carols are playing from a little stereo system. The room is drenched in loving gifts from a wealthy city to a poor family.

But that's not the miracle.

Perfecta, Lydia, and Jenny are busy packing many of their gifts back up. As they write the names of friends on the boxes you blurt out, "What are you doing? Why are you giving your gifts away?" You think of your own Christmas — all the new stuff under the tree that you would never think of giving away.

Perfecta says gently, "Our neighbors are still in need. We cannot have plenty while they have nothing. This is what Jesus likes us to do." You just stare, your eyes wide. The grandmother continues, her eyes tender. "We did nothing to deserve these gifts. But the greatest gift of all is the one we're celebrating today: the gift of Jesus."

You have a lot to think about on the ride home. The Delgados were happy when they were poor and when they were showered with gifts. But instead of hoarding their gifts for a rainy day, their first thought was to share. Why? They said it had to do with Jesus — what he "likes us" to do. Just as if he were right here, a living person!

You think about the story your family always

tells at Christmas, about the little baby in the manger — two thousand years ago, right? Exactly who was in that manger? Can he make you as beautiful inside as the Delgados are?

There was something in the old story about shepherds. An angel told them a baby had been born nearby, and the shepherds said, "Hey, let's go check it out."

Let's do the same. Who was in the manger? Is he real? And how can we be sure?

Let's go check it out!

Part 1
WHO WAS IN THE MANGER?

Chapter 1

WHO DID THIS GUY THINK HE WAS?

D id you know there is life on the moon?

Back in 1835, a newspaper called the *New York Sun* printed an entire series of articles claiming that life had just been discovered on the moon. A famous scientist named Sir John Herschel was said to have rigged up a really effective new telescope. He could peer through its lens and see exactly what was happening up on the lunar surface. He said he had spotted buffalo, goats, unicorns, and even winged humanoids building temples!

Also, it seemed as if the moon would make a terrific vacation site. There were beaches, oceans, and forests up there. You could enjoy them as you took a walk in the earthlight.

Some people got pretty excited. But when someone checked with Sir John Herschel, the whole story fell apart. He said he didn't have a new telescope and he had no idea what was on the moon. But he *did* have a good laugh!

This was what we call a "hoax" today — a story created to attract attention. The crazy story made the *Sun* a very popular paper, even after everyone found out the truth. But it just goes to show: Don't believe everything you read. When you hear a wild claim, find out the truth for yourself. See if the story holds up.

You've heard a lot about Jesus — the guy who was born in a manger and died on the cross to save you from your sins. Why not see if the story of Jesus holds up? After all, it's a bigger deal than goats on the moon. Some people think he was simply a nice guy and a good teacher. He was just a regular person who taught people to live by the Golden Rule. Others think he never lived at all. Still others believe he was something more than "regular." They say he was the Son of God, and that we should love him and follow him in all that we do.

> **GOLDEN RULE:** treating others the same way you would like to be treated

There are a lot of differences in those ideas, aren't there? You need to decide for yourself what you think about Jesus. It isn't enough to repeat something you've heard without thinking about it yourself. There are several points for you to look at. First, what did Jesus say about himself? Was he crazy or dishonest? And how much evidence is there to support the amazing claims people make about him? Nearly all of Christians' ideas about Jesus come from the Bible, but how do you know those Bible stories are true? And last but most important, there is the matter of Christ coming back from the dead. It's the single most important claim anyone can make about Jesus.

WHAT DID THE MAN SAY ABOUT HIMSELF?

Most of our information about Jesus comes from one book: the Bible. Historians have found more than one hundred stories about Jesus in other ancient writings, but the Bible is still the most complete source of information about him. So it's important to figure out whether the Bible can be trusted. What if that book is wrong? If somebody proves that the Bible is made up, that casts a lot of doubt on Jesus. In a few pages we'll take a close look at that question. But for now, let's go to the stories and simply find out what Jesus said.

HISTORIAN: someone who studies events that have taken place in the past. Historians have found facts about Jesus in writings from scholars like Josephus and Pliny the Younger.

All of the stories about Jesus are found in four books called the "Gospels" (which means "good news"). One of the Gospels is called John. Listen to what it says about Jesus. It calls him "the Word."

In the beginning, the Word was already there. The Word was with God, and the Word was God. He was with God in the beginning. All things were made through him. Nothing that has been made was made without him... The Word became a human being. He made his home with us. We have seen his glory. It is the glory of the one and only Son.

John 1:1–3, 14

Stop! Time out! "The Word"? Jesus didn't *say* a word here! This is other people making a big deal about him. If he's something special, we should hear it from his *own* lips. Otherwise it would seem that people made claims about him that he never intended.

Surely he didn't go around calling himself "the Word" or "the One and Only." So we turn over to the longest Gospel, the one called Matthew. It has a whole lot of statements from Jesus' own mouth.

Here's a passage that comes right to the point. Jesus asks his friends, "Who do you say I am?" His friend Peter says that Jesus is "the Christ ... the Son of the living God." Again, these people seem eager to make a big deal.

But Jesus does *not* act embarrassed, like he would have if that hadn't been true. Far from it! He seems very pleased by Peter's words, and he says, "No mere man showed this to you. My Father in heaven showed it to you" (Matthew 16:15–17).

And back in John's Gospel they're having still another conversation about this subject. Somebody asks Jesus, "If you are the Christ, tell us plainly." Here is how Jesus answers: "I and the Father are one."

It's right there in John 10, verses 24 and 30.

If you read a little closer, you find that this was the kind of remark that could get you into hot water — because once they heard this, the men around Jesus said "'You are only a man. But you claim to be God'"(verse 33). And then they picked up rocks to throw at him!

Jesus called himself ...

The way and the truth and the life (John 14:6)
King of the Jews (Luke 23:3)
Bread of life (John 6:35)
The Messiah (John 4:25 - 26)
God's Son (John 10:36)
The good shepherd (John 10:11)
The true vine (John 15:1)
The light of the world (John 8:12)

Question: Is it bragging to use "big names" for yourself as Jesus did? What would make doing this boastful or not boastful?

I'LL BELIEVE IT WHEN I SEE IT

So the Bible tells us that Jesus said he was one with the Father. Are you still not so sure about all this? It's hard to trust someone else's word. And guess what? There's another guy like that a few pages later! His name was Thomas, and he was one of Jesus' disciples (his closest friends and followers). When the other disciples told him that Jesus had risen from the dead, Thomas said that he'd believe it as soon as he saw and touched the cuts and scars on Jesus' hands and feet.

Thomas got his wish! Jesus turned up, gave a show-and-tell of the wounds he'd received on the cross, and Thomas said, "My Lord and my God!" (John 20:28). Then Jesus said, "You believe because you see me. Those who believe without seeing me will be truly happy" (John 20:29 NCV).

We all want to be truly happy. But it's still expecting a lot for us to believe this man was God just because he said he was. On the other hand, after looking at the Bible we have to admit one thing: Jesus made some mighty big claims about himself. He wasn't at all shy about calling himself One with God — or about letting his friends call him such things.

Well, Jesus talked the talk. So what? Maybe

he wasn't telling the truth. He wouldn't be the first guy to stretch the truth a little. Let's consider that point.

WAS JESUS LYING ABOUT HIMSELF?

You've known people who exaggerated their own abilities: "I can beat that video game in one day." Or, "I'm the smartest kid at school." People usually stretch the truth in order to get something they want — usually respect or attention. What about Jesus? What did he have to gain by lying about who he was? What benefit did he get by saying he was God's son if he was only a man?

We've already seen one answer to that: rocks! In those days, you could be stoned to death just for saying the wrong thing. People had to speak *very* carefully. In Mark's Gospel, Jesus was put on trial because of the things he had said. They put him on the spot: "Are you the Christ? Are you the Son of the Blessed One?" (Mark 14:61). And he replied, "I am" (verse 62). Jesus has seen people beaten and crucified. He knows there are many people who want to kill him. He knows the consequences of speaking this way. But he's sticking to what he knows to be the truth.

Now think about the kid who lies about his video game skills. Would he stick to his story if a whole mob of kids threatened to attack him because of his words? That's what Jesus was threatened with: terrible beatings and then death. He insisted on his claim, and they insisted on killing him.

So what have you learned?
Jesus claimed to be God.
That claim got him killed.

Question: Would you die for a lie?
Do you think Jesus would have done so?

Chapter 2

WAS JESUS OUT OF HIS MIND?

L ots of insane people walk around claiming to be God. Jesus might have been too crazy to say the right thing and save his own life. How would you know?

You could watch his behavior closely. You would expect an insane person's actions to give him away.

You're not an expert on how crazy people act. But a professor named Dr. Gary Collins can help. He has spent his career working with those who have mental disorders of all kinds. He offers us a list of some of the main signs of insanity. We can study his list, then take a good look at whether Jesus acted like a crazy person:

Symptom of Insanity	Action of Jesus
Unpredictable emotion; depression or anger at odd times	Jesus wept when his friend died and became angry when he saw people cheating the poor.
Imagining people are out to get you	Jesus did believe a friend was out to get him — and he was right.
Thinking problems; trouble carrying on long conversations	Jesus' sermons were orderly and logical.

Does he sound crazy to you? Wouldn't you cry if one of your friends died? Or if you saw someone stealing from a poor person? Jesus kept things interesting — no doubt about that. But he never showed any of the classic signs of insanity. He reacted pretty normally in all of these situations. Here's evidence that some people thought he was out of his mind:

> A lot of them were saying, "He's crazy, a maniac — out of his head completely. Why bother listening to him?" But others weren't so sure: "These aren't the words of a crazy man. Can a 'maniac' open blind eyes?"
> John 10:20 – 21 MSG

Well, they had a point! Your average crazy person doesn't heal blind people, walk on water, or feed five thousand people from one basket. Many people said they saw Jesus do these things. Crazy people don't perform miracles; they act crazy.

Miracles. They're a pretty important part of all this, aren't they? As we read these Gospels, you can see that Jesus used miracles to show who he really was. They would be pretty good evidence

... if they were real, that is. After all, you don't often see people walking on water or controlling storms. If the miracles were not real, then that's also evidence. It would mean Jesus was a fake.

These miracles are worth looking into.

MAYBE HE WAS A GREAT HYPNOTIST

Perhaps you could hypnotize someone to think you were walking on water or controlling the weather. A good hypnotist could give you water and make you think you were drinking soda. Maybe that was how Jesus pulled off that trick where he seemed to change water into wine.

Let's compare Jesus' miracles to hypnotism:

Hypnotism	Miracles
Many people in an audience are resistant to hypnotism.	Jesus performed miracles in huge crowds.
People can usually be hypnotized only when they're willing.	Many of Jesus' enemies saw the miracles. They weren't willing at all!
Hypnotists need words. They can't hypnotize without speaking.	When Jesus changed water into wine, he never spoke to the people drinking it.

So, hypnotism doesn't really fit. There were simply too many witnesses. Jesus spoke to large, active crowds. That meant he had to speak up, instead of softly the way you hear hypnotists talk in movies. He didn't choose certain ideal subjects, but performed miracles everyone could see (including people who didn't want to see miracles at all). Sometimes he even performed miracles that happened miles away! (See John 4:43–54, for instance.) No one can hypnotize someone in the next town.

There was no doubt Jesus was more than just a simple teacher: he was one who calmly and sanely claimed to be God, performed miracles, and died for his claim.

But remember that word Peter called him — "the Christ"? Some think that was just his last name: Mr. Christ. But last names don't make so many people angry, as the use of "Christ" did with Jesus. People seemed as upset about this title as the one "God's Son."

The word *Christ* means "Messiah." Okay, that's helpful. What's *that* one mean?

Chapter 3

MESSIAH: DID JESUS FIT THE PICTURE?

The Jews expected a great hero called the Messiah to save them one day. The Old Testament had a lot to say about what the Messiah might be like, which gives us a chance to see how Jesus stacked up to that job description. If he fit all the qualifications that the Jews had set out for the Messiah long before he was born, that would be even more evidence in Jesus' favor.

Messiah: Ancient Superhero?

The Jews, Jesus' people, believed that God would send a special person to rescue everyone. Throughout the Old Testament of the Bible, you will find many clues and hints about this hero who would come. The Jews were very eager to meet their Messiah, but they were not sure when to expect him. Jesus claimed he was that special Savior.

Question: If a great new hero arrived in today's world, what do you think he would be like? What kinds of things would he spend his time on?

You will find references to the Messiah all through the Old Testament, usually in the books of the prophets — people who preached about God and sometimes told what God had in store for the future. Finding the Messiah in the Old Testament is like an Easter egg hunt. There's a clue hidden here, another one there, and yet another detail hidden somewhere else.

It takes a good while to make the full "hunt" and get the whole picture. But there were certain details about this coming deliverer that many Jewish people knew. It was known that he would be born in Bethlehem. He would be descended from David. He would bring a brand new kingdom for Israel, the greatest ever. He would set up his kingdom to last forever.

The box below offers a particularly clear picture of this mysterious Savior.

The Messiah will be faced with these challenges:

Men looked down on him. They didn't accept him. He knew all about sorrow and suffering... But the servant was pierced because we had sinned... He was punished to make us whole again. His wounds have healed us... He took the sins of many people on himself. And he gave his life for those who had done what is wrong.
(Isaiah 53:3, 5, 12)

Sound familiar? Yes, it would be hard to come up with a better word picture of the Jesus you know from the New Testament. According to Isaiah, a prophet who lived hundreds of years before Jesus was born, the Messiah would be unpopular with many people and would suffer greatly. Though not doing anything wrong or hurting anyone, he would be "pierced because we had sinned." That means he would accept the punishment (through some sharp weapon) for other people's wrongdoings. He would die among wicked people but be buried among the rich. And because of his wounds, our own hurts would be healed.

From the Gospels, we know that Jesus was indeed unpopular among the religious leaders at the time he was killed. Crowds yelled for his execution. We know he suffered, and that he was pierced with nails and crucified (this punishment was not used in Isaiah's time). He never did anything wrong, never hurt anyone, but died for our wrongs so that we could be healed. It all checks out!

You might think, "That's cool, but it couldn't have been written *before* Jesus lived." As a matter of fact, it was. Seven hundred years before Jesus, to be exact! It is impossible that it could have been faked, because we know that those precise words of Isaiah (and the other prophets too) have been there all along, and never changed.

Question: The way you see it, which prediction about the Messiah fits Jesus best? How come?

FIVE DOZEN REASONS

All in all, there are about sixty important predictions about Jesus in the Old Testament. Remember, the prophets were giving details of someone who would not be born for hundreds of years!

Okay, so how about this for an explanation? Jesus knew all those Scriptures. Could it be that he used the predictions as a kind of road map, and went along with following their demands?

The only problem is that there were many prophecy fulfillments he *couldn't* arrange — such as being born in the town of Bethlehem. Micah 5:2 nailed that one. He couldn't arrange to be betrayed for a specific amount of money (Zechariah

11:12–13), or for men to gamble to see who got to keep his clothing (Psalm 22:18).

Well, what about coincidence? Why couldn't there have been several people who fulfilled those prophecies? Jesus might have just been the one who got all the credit. But a science professor named Dr. Peter Stoner says that's highly unlikely. He and six hundred students wanted to find out the likelihood of someone fulfilling so many prophecies. They came up with very reasonable estimates and used a lot of complicated math equations (you don't want to know!) to figure out that the chances of any one person fulfilling just *eight* of the prophecies was one in a hundred million billion.

Maybe all those figures are wrong. You do the math (or not). Think about this example alone. David wrote, "A group of sinful people has closed in on me. They are all around me like a pack of dogs. They have pierced my hands and feet … They laugh when I suffer. They divide up my clothes among them. They cast lots for what I am wearing"

COINCIDENCE: events that happen at the same time accidentally but seem to have a connection

(Psalm 22:16–18). David, who lived long before the Romans and their practice of crucifixion, was writing the thoughts of his own descendant, about one thousand years before that descendant (Jesus) would be born! It seems like too much to be a simple coincidence, doesn't it?

Fitting the Big Picture		
	Old Testament Prophecy	New Testament Fulfillment
Birthplace	Bethlehem (Micah 5:2)	Bethlehem (Matthew 2:1)
Family	David's line (Jeremiah 23:5–6)	David's line (Matthew 1)
Blood Money	30 pieces of silver (Zechariah 11:12–13)	30 pieces of silver (Matthew 26:15)
Gambling for Clothing	Cast lots for clothing (Psalm 22:18)	Cast lots for clothing (Matthew 27:35)

WHAT ARE THE ODDS?

Jesus knew the importance of all those ancient predictions. He said, "Everything written about me in the Law of Moses, the Prophets and the Psalms must come true" (Luke 24:44). He was certainly aware that he was fulfilling the predictions, but could he have arranged for so many to fit? And if so, why would he do it, knowing his reward would be a cross on a hill?

When Jesus was arrested, he was in a garden praying that there might be some way for him not to face such an awful death. "My soul is very sad. I feel close to death," he said to his friends who were also in the garden. Then he prayed, "My Father, if it is possible, take this cup of suffering away from me. But let what you want be done, not what I want" (Matthew 26:38–39). He was not eager to suffer, but would do exactly what his Father wanted him to do.

So what do you think?

Do these sound like the words and actions of a crazy person? A faker? What's your take?

Question: So we've looked at what Jesus said and what he did. What did you find most surprising in this section? What did you find most interesting? Why?

If we can trust the Bible, the picture it presents of Jesus is fascinating. If the Gospels are true, there has never been anyone in the world like Jesus. But those are big ifs. The Bible could be a collection of fairy tales. It could be a bunch of deliberate lies. It could be a mistake.

Couldn't it?

Part 2

DID HIS FRIENDS TELL THE TRUTH?

Chapter 4

DON'T BELIEVE EVERYTHING YOU READ

So you're with your mom, waiting in the checkout line at the grocery store. There are magazines and a couple of colorful newspapers. Wow! Look at the news! It's been a busy day for current events. Aliens have abducted the president of the United States and replaced him with a body double. A wolf-boy has been found roaming the woods of Montana. You think of the story about unicorns and winged humans running around on the moon.

With amazing news like this, shouldn't you buy those papers? But Mom says, "Don't believe everything you read."

Parents like to say that because ... well, it's true. Being written down doesn't make something true. And that's exactly where we find ourselves in searching for the truth about Jesus. The Bible's claims about Jesus are *much* more incredible than any claim about a wolf-boy in Montana. The Bible's claims are about miracles, reversing death, and fulfilling seven-hundred-year-old prophecies. There's enough stuff there to keep the grocery store papers busy for months.

The claims are written down, but are they trustworthy?

COUNTING THE EYEBALLS

When an event is in question, investigators ask, "How many eyeballs were there?"

In other words, how many people saw the event? To believe something happened, we need witnesses to trust — and the more of them, the better. How many eyeballs can back up Jesus' story? If it was only one guy who came up with the whole saga, we would all be suspicious.

But the story of Jesus comes from *four* different authors: Matthew, Mark, Luke, and John. We call them the Gospels, which is a word meaning *good news*. But was it news at all, or was it pretending to be news? You have to study them closely to decide.

John, for example, was a disciple. His eyeballs were on the scene, and he is eager for us to understand that. He says he is telling us about things "which we have heard, which we have seen with our eyes, which we have looked at and our hands have touched" (1 John 1:1 NIV).

Luke is a first-rate reporter, offering plenty of checkable details. Listen to what he says: "I myself have carefully looked into everything from the beginning. So it seemed good also to me to write an orderly report of exactly what happened" (Luke 1:3). Then there's Mark, who got much of his account from Peter, a particularly close friend of Jesus.

By the way, Peter's story is not just in Mark — it's also in his own writings. He says, "We didn't make up stories when we told you about it. With our own eyes we saw him in all his majesty" (2 Peter 1:16).

What They Wrote and Why	
Matthew:	Disciple of Jesus. Wrote to show Jewish readers how Jesus fulfilled the old prophecies.
Mark:	Close friend of the disciple Peter. First of the four to write a Gospel. Eager to tell the simple facts.
Luke:	A doctor who was a companion of Paul, an eyewitness of the resurrected Jesus. Luke talked to Mary and many others, making a full and careful investigation of what happened.
John:	Disciple who wanted to share the facts that showed Jesus was the Son of God.

Are you surprised that the Gospel writers *expected* people to have questions about their amazing stories? They were careful to show that their accounts came from eyewitnesses: the disciples, the people who were healed, those who heard Jesus' teachings, and even Mary and Joseph who raised Jesus.

WHAT ABOUT THEIR DIFFERENCES?

Here's another question. Do the Gospel writers agree on all the details? Well, they do provide different perspectives. So isn't that a big problem? If these four couldn't get their stories straight, what are you supposed to think?

PERSPECTIVE: someone's point of view of a subject or an event. For example, the boy's perspective of exactly what happened in a big football play is based on the location of his seat in the stadium.

It happens all the time. Imagine four people see an automobile accident on Main Street. There are going to be little differences in their stories of what they saw happen. Who is right? Or are all of them wrong?

Here's something surprising about testimony differences. History experts say that little variations make a story more believable! Why? Because that's life. We all see things from different positions. People tend to be clear about the main thing that they see — for instance, which car rammed into the other one. But they also miss little things (for instance, what color shirts the drivers were wearing). History books are filled with different perspectives among people who were there for wars and other great events. But when it comes to who won the battle and what the main events were, they are on the same page.

Whose Side of the Story?

Someone reports a fight in the school cafeteria. Four kids are questioned about the incident – but their stories don't quite match!

Does this mean:

A. The fight never happened?
B. There's one honest kid and three liars?
C. All are truthful but had different perspectives?

If you think about it, most of the time the answer is "C." Observers emphasize different details. The little variations make them more believable, not less so.

Question: When you hear different stories, how do you decide who is telling the truth? What kinds of things do you consider?

This is certainly the case with the four Gospels. On every key point, they agree. On the little things, they sometimes offer different perspectives and details.

Chapter 5

IT'S A CONSPIRACY!

Let's try another one. Maybe Matthew, Mark, Luke, and John were four guys who entered into a conspiracy. Maybe they really wanted their new church to be successful, so they agreed to make up a story and stick to it. Maybe it was all a

CONSPIRACY: an agreement between people who are trying to cover up something they did that was wrong or illegal

big prank. Could that explain the stories of Jesus?

To repeat our last point, if they had made up the story, their accounts would have been suspiciously consistent. But there's a larger point. People tend to lie when there is something to be gained. Your classmate might claim her father is a millionaire, for instance. Rewards? Friends would be impressed. They would invite her to more parties. (The lie is unlikely to succeed for very long, of course.)

How about Matthew, Mark, Luke, and John? Was a more successful church their reward? History clearly tells us that early Christians were rewarded with … *death*. Christianity wasn't too popular with public leaders for a few centuries. Most of the disciples were killed by people who were angry about these stories of a dead man who rose again. So if the Gospel writers were lying,

CONSISTENT: when two or more sides of the story are exactly the same

they did so at the strong risk of death. Do you think they would lie under those conditions?

Another reason lying would be unlikely is the painful account of Jesus. The gospel writers told how people jeered at him and wanted him to die. They told the manner of his death. Crucifixion was considered a mark of shame in those days. Paul wrote, "But we preach about Christ and his death on the cross. That is very hard for Jews to accept. And everyone else thinks it's foolish" (1 Corinthians 1:23). Why make up a story that people won't accept or will think is foolish?

FACT CHECKERS

Magazines hire "fact checkers." These are people who carefully check all the facts and make sure mistakes don't slip into the news story.

The four Gospels were surrounded by fact checkers, so how could they lie? People were still alive who could remember seeing Jesus in person. If these amazing stories had been lies, wouldn't there have been many people coming forward to set the record straight?

But shortly after Jesus was killed, Peter talked to a large crowd about "miracles, wonders and signs among you through Jesus. You yourselves know this." He went on to say, "God has raised this same Jesus back to life. We are all witnesses of this" (Acts 2:22, 32).

That's about the same as you saying, "I transformed into a giant eggplant last Tuesday in the school cafeteria, and you saw it yourself." You couldn't get away with saying something like that *unless* it really happened. The only people likely to believe a wild story are those who saw it and know it's true. And Peter wrote about Jesus to such people.

As a matter of fact, we are told that when Peter talked to that crowd, three thousand people took his advice and became followers of Christ. Jesus was mighty popular for a "dead" man! You can read the whole story in Acts 2. It's a wild one!

What Paul said about it ...

I passed on to you... Christ died for our sins, just as Scripture said he would. He was buried. He was raised from the dead on the third day. He appeared to Peter. Then he appeared to the Twelve. After that, he appeared to more than 500 believers at the same time. Most of them are still living. (1 Corinthians 15:3 – 6)

Question: Would thousands of people have become Christians if the disciples were making up wild stories?

REPLAY

You've learned a lot so far. The Gospels cannot be easily dismissed as made-up stories or lies. There is too much good evidence and common sense on the other side of the question. We also know that the story of Jesus has stood the test of time. For two thousand years, no one has been successful in disproving it. That's a pretty strong record.

The story is so strong because it was told by eyewitnesses who were willing to die for their story. Jesus didn't seem to be a liar, act like a crazy person, or try to hypnotize people. Neither did the people who followed him. Smart people believed in him, and smart people still believe in him today.

The question is, so what? If a man performed miracles twenty centuries ago, why should that be a big deal today? Imagine someone discovering tomorrow that dinosaurs still walk the earth in a remote corner of South America. It would be a big story, there would be TV reports, but what happens after the surprise wears off? Wouldn't we all just go back to what we were doing before they found the big reptiles?

The difference is that many people *still* follow

Jesus. They seem to find that following Jesus makes their lives better. It makes them happier even when times are rough, as with the Delgados you read about at the beginning of the book. It gives them answers for their questions about how to live. Following Jesus gives them a friendship like no other.

If Jesus could do miracles then, and if death is no problem for him — can he do miracles now? The only thing to do is keep on the trail. It's time to investigate the biggest question of all: whether a person can come back from the dead.

Question: The way you see it, what does believing in Jesus have to do with the way you live and treat others? How come?

Part 3

CAN A DEAD MAN COME BACK?

Chapter 6

COMING BACK FROM THE DEAD?

Hey, it happens every day.

At least, it happens on television. For example, think about the story *Pinocchio*. A wooden puppet comes back to life as a real boy. The Beast in *Beauty and the Beast*, killed in a fight, comes back to life as a handsome prince.

Snow White, Sleeping Beauty — dead one minute, off to a wedding the next. In all kinds of stories, there's nothing more exciting and dramatic than a *resurrection*.

RESURRECTION:
when someone comes
back to life after dying

But that's kid stuff, right? Fairy-tale material. Or it's even *more* unbelievable, like in a scary movie. A mummy that comes to life and chases people around. Resurrection never happens in the real world. Or does it?

Well, this is the big question when we talk about Jesus. Christians insist that Jesus did exactly that. They say that he died, was buried, then rose after three days in his tomb. They say that he offered the same power over death to his followers. That's what the good news is all about: not having to be afraid of death.

If you think about it, even Christ's greatest miracles would have been forgotten otherwise.

Question: The Bible says Jesus walked on water and stopped a big storm. Is that a bigger deal than reviving after death, in your opinion? What makes resurrection so special?

NOT QUITE DEAD

If you heard that a man fell down dead, then got up and walked away, what would be your first thought? You might blurt out, "He wasn't really dead! He was just knocked out."

There are a few of these "after death" stories from time to time. In the hospital, patients can be pronounced dead, only to revive a moment or two later. We understand, of course, that these people did not *really* die. It just seemed that way to the doctors.

That's what many people have suggested about Jesus. It seems more believable than really coming back from the dead, doesn't it? Jesus died on a Roman cross. But maybe in this one case, the guys didn't get the job done. Maybe they pulled him down a little early, laid him in the cave, and went home to dinner. Later on, Jesus opened his eyes, feeling a little weak and sore. When he returned to his friends, they just assumed it was a miracle — that he had really come back from the dead. Then they could say, "Hey, he really is the Messiah after all!"

Or say ... maybe it was no accident at all, but one more part of Jesus' make-the-prophecies-happen plan. Maybe Jesus took a special knock-out drug that would make him seem dead for a couple of days. He faked his own death, knowing all along that coming back would make him a big sensation.

Let's take a closer look at these not-quite-dead theories.

DID HE FAKE THE WHOLE THING?

The fake-death crowd offers three items of evidence to support their view:

- Mark 15:36 says that on the cross, Jesus was offered some drink on a sponge. A drug?
- Mark 15:44 says Pilate was surprised by Jesus' quick death. Was he buried too quickly?
- Jesus walked and talked later. Could it be he never died at all?

But now let's look at the other side. Those two verses from Mark are interesting — but a good investigator must consider *all* the evidence.

BLOOD, SWEAT, AND TEARS. Remember when Jesus went to pray in the garden? He wept and prayed, and "his sweat was like drops of blood" (Luke 22:44). That's a pretty strange diagnosis from a doctor, wouldn't you think? When was the last time you had bloody sweat?

Turns out Luke was a good doctor after all. Today we know about a rare condition (hematohidrosis) that matches Luke's description. And what causes this bloody sweat? Grief and anxiety. Blood goes right into the sweat glands.

STRIPPED AND WHIPPED. Jesus received a severe beating at the hands of the Roman guards. They would have removed his clothing and used a whip of braided leather with sharp things woven in. So terrible was this torture that some victims never even made it to the cross.

Why is this important? It tells us that Jesus would have been in a very serious medical condition before he even made it up to the cross. Hold that thought for a moment.

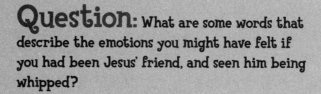

Question: What are some words that describe the emotions you might have felt if you had been Jesus' friend, and seen him being whipped?

Rated V for Violent

The truth about crucifixion is shocking, isn't it? You can see just how painful and terrible it was for Jesus. Yet he stayed in Jerusalem, knowing these things would happen to him! Why would he do that? Christians believe he was willing to accept a painful death so that God would forgive the sins (or wrongs) of all those who love Jesus and understand what he did for them. In other words, he was volunteering for the punishment the rest of us would earn for all our sins throughout our lives. How does that make you feel about Jesus?

Chapter 7

A BODY ON THE CROSS

Most of us have seen pictures of Jesus on a cross, but those images usually don't tell the whole story. The cross remains one of the cruelest torture methods ever invented. It was slow, painful, and terrible in every way.

First there were the thick spikes (not thin little nails). When hammered through the wrist, they would have damaged the large nerve that enters the hand. The cross would then be thrust into the earth before the ankles received the same treatment.

The weight of the victim's body, pulling against the nails, would have extended his arms by about six inches, according to scientists.

Death came from a combination of factors. Hanging in this position, a victim would have to push up with his feet to breathe. After pushing up too much, the victim would be very tired. The heart would beat irregularly, and death would come through lack of breathing, heart failure, and exhaustion. The information the Gospels give fits all the facts that modern doctors know about this kind of death.

FOUND IN A CAVE

Critics once claimed that crucifixion as described in the Gospels was impossible. They said that nails or even spikes would not support the weight of a body. But in 1968, in a cave near Jerusalem, the remains of a crucified body were found. The male was in his twenties, and his wounds matched the descriptions of Jesus' wounds.

MORE ABOUT CRUCIFIXION

Many ancient cultures used crucifixion as a way to execute people, but the Romans did so for nearly one thousand years. On one occasion, after stopping a slave revolt led by a man named Spartacus, the Romans crucified six thousand rebels at one time.

PUT IT ALL TOGETHER

Now, think about what you learned about the whipping that would have left Jesus terribly injured. Think about the nerves to the hands being destroyed, as well as the difficulty in breathing. If Jesus somehow survived all of this by being taken from the cross a little early — what kind of shape do you think he would have been in three days later?

He wouldn't have appeared fit and healthy as the Gospels tell us he appeared. Instead, he would have looked gruesome! The disciples would have called a doctor, not launched a worldwide movement based on the wonderful claim that they would someday overcome death as Jesus did.

To believe Jesus didn't die on the cross, you must choose certain facts in the Gospel and ignore others — and that's not a very effective way to come to the most accurate conclusion.

WAS THE TOMB REALLY EMPTY?

Being realistic, we must agree that Jesus could not have survived the execution described in his four biographies. So the whole question comes down to his burial place, doesn't it? Either that tomb held the body of a dead Jewish teacher or it didn't.

So ... was the tomb really empty? Remember, people were saying, "Jesus is alive! He must be the Son of God!" And what would you have expected Jesus' enemies to say? If the dead body had still been there, they could have brought it out and quickly and easily dried up all the excitement. But in Matthew 28:13, the leaders only said, "They stole his body while we were sleeping." In other words, they admitted it was missing.

Question: Why do you think the leaders of Jesus' time were so intent on discouraging Jesus' followers? Why do you think some people today might feel the same way?

SO WAS THE BODY STOLEN?

Maybe the religious leaders were right. Many skeptical people have tried to claim that Jesus' followers stole the body then claimed a resurrection. But let's think about what this would have required.

Jesus was not buried in a hole in the ground, but a cave — actually a tiny room cut out of rock. A large, disk-shaped rock blocked the one small entrance. You could easily roll the rock downhill into place, but it would take many strong men to roll it back up. So a great deal of organized effort was required.

Also, the tomb was guarded. Matthew 27:63–66 tells us that Jesus' enemies were worried that the body would be stolen to fulfill Jesus' prediction that he would rise after three days.

Take some guards with you," Pilate answered. "Go. Make the tomb as secure as you can." So they went and made the tomb secure. They put a seal on the stone and placed some guards on duty.
(Matthew 27: 65 – 66)

So highly trained Roman guards stood by the tomb. Do you think it would have been easy for a few of Jesus' friends to get by them and break in? Remember, they would have run a very high risk of being beaten and crucified.

Would the Romans have stolen the body? They had no reason to do so.

Would the religious leaders have stolen the body? As we have seen, they took measures to keep the body from being stolen.

Question: What conclusion do you draw about whether Jesus really died? What conclusion do you draw about what happened to his body?

WHAT ABOUT THE DISCIPLES?

There is one other piece to the resurrection puzzle. Why would the disciples change so much in their courage and hope?

When Jesus was arrested, they went into hiding. They were afraid that they would be arrested too. Even when they heard the first reports that Jesus was not in his tomb, they were reluctant to believe. "But the apostles did not believe the women. Their words didn't make any sense to them" (Luke 24:11). Like most of the world, they considered the idea of rising from the dead to be ridiculous.

But something happened. Within a few years, the same disciples were leading a movement that spread all across the Roman Empire — even though many believers were punished or killed for joining it. Of the eleven remaining disciples (Judas, the betrayer, was dead), Christian history records that ten were executed for their faith. Their belief gave them that much courage.

Question: How strongly would you have to believe something to give your life for it? Why do you think the disciples were so convinced?

Chapter 8
THE FURTHER ADVENTURES OF JESUS

Elvis Presley was a rock star. During the 1950s, he was the most popular singer in America. And his fans continued to buy each of his records and see each of his movies long after his death in 1977.

Many of those fans were so devoted to Elvis they just couldn't believe that he was dead. Over the years, "Elvis sightings" have been reported in grocery store tabloids (the kind of newspapers that have alien and wolf-boy stories). There have been jokes and even movies about finding Elvis as alive as ever. People have fun imagining, but they don't really believe he is alive. Why?

Simply because there isn't any good evidence that he isn't still in his grave.

What about Jesus? There were "Jesus sightings," but couldn't they have been like the wolf-boy tales of their time? Couldn't they have been legends and tall tales?

The Gospels give us several stories of public appearances made by Jesus after his burial. Our job is to decide whether those stories are believable.

HOW ABOUT FIVE HUNDRED EYEWITNESSES?

The most dramatic report of a Jesus sighting is found in a letter by Paul the Apostle. In 1 Corinthians 15:3–6, Paul lists the evidence for his readers. He says that Jesus died, was buried, and rose after three days, just as the prophecies had said. Paul affirmed that Jesus "appeared to Peter, and then to the Twelve. After that, he appeared to more than five hundred of the brothers at the same time, most of whom are still living" (verses 5–6 NIV).

In other words, the world was still filled with people who had seen and spoken with a resurrected

Jesus! Paul wrote this letter knowing that many would pass it around. Do you think he would have made such a statement if it could be easily disproved? He basically said, "Plenty of folks saw and spoke to Jesus. Ask them yourself!"

URBAN LEGEND?

Have you heard of urban legends? They're stories that are passed around and believed, but aren't true. There is an urban legend that the sewers of New York City have crocodiles! That one has been disproved many times. Couldn't the Jesus sightings be urban legends of their time?

The main problem with this theory is that there wasn't enough time for a legend to grow. Scholars and historians tell us that legends (such as the stories of King Arthur or Robin Hood) take hundreds of years to develop. They also begin small and grow larger. But Paul wrote his account about five hundred eyewitnesses before the Gospels were written. As he said, he was writing within the lifetime of eyewitnesses. The shocking claim of a resurrection would quickly be disproved — unless it were true.

Also, myths and urban legends never "name names." You can never find someone who actually witnessed the event that is claimed. But Paul and the gospel writers offered names, places, and details

for Jesus' appearances. And remember, Luke was a doctor and a serious historian who was committed to investigation and truth.

HALLUCINATIONS?

Some people have suggested that the disciples were so emotionally overcome that they began "seeing things." They missed Jesus so deeply that they imagined him back with them.

But experts on hallucinations insist that they are not a group activity. People have individual hallucinations — not in groups of eleven or of five hundred. And once again, wouldn't they have gone to the grave and checked? Wouldn't an occupied tomb have cured their hallucinations?

Finally, remember that these disciples — and many early Christians — were willing to die for this idea. Would they have died for a hallucination or something that was not totally convincing?

HALLUCINATIONS:
seeing people or things
that aren't really there

EVEN MORE ADVENTURES OF JESUS

There is only one more avenue of evidence — that of Jesus continuing to walk and talk with believers.

Evidence from the past is very important. But what about evidence that is still fresh? Perhaps the greatest reason of all for the faith of hundreds of millions of Christians around the world is that they know Jesus as a friend, right now. There is a character in American legends named Paul Bunyan. It would be easy to convince you that he never actually lived ... mostly because he didn't. But if you have a good friend who goes to school with you and talks to you on the phone, it would be *very* difficult to convince you that he didn't exist!

That's the way many people are with Jesus. They believe he once lived, once died, once rose again, and still lives today. They know it because they talk to him in prayer every day. They know it because they can feel his presence with them as they go about their daily lives. And they know it because he has brought many good changes to their lives.

The Delgados, from way back at the beginning of this book, were people like that. They lived the way they knew Jesus wanted them to live, and it made them happier in every way. It caused good things and tough things in life to make sense. And they knew that when they had a problem or a challenge of any kind, Jesus would be there to love and help them. Through his teachings in the Bible, Jesus offers wonderful advice for every problem to people like the Delgados — and to you.

They also knew that life's greatest fear — death — can be managed because Jesus rose from the dead two thousand years ago. The evidence is convincing: Jesus was telling the truth when he said that whoever believed in him would not die but have eternal life. (See John 3:16.)

In other words, the story of Jesus is not a fairy tale. But it does have one thing in common with those stories: it has a happy ending. Jesus has promised that no matter what you face, there will be a happy ending for you. And when you know that, you have a whole new attitude about life — an attitude of excitement and hope.

WHAT NOW?

So where do you go from here?

Imagine you're just the way you were at the beginning of the book. You were taking a walk when you became lost and found the Delgados. But this time you have found someone else.

You ask him, "Where to now?"

He smiles and puts a hand around your shoulder. As he does so, you see the scar on his wrist left by a nail long ago. He says, "Where do you want to go?"

You reply, "Well, I thought I was lost ..."

And he says, "That's one of the good things! There are many roads to take. Some lead home, and some lead to new adventures. But whichever road you take, I will go with you. I will always be available to encourage you and care for you. That's what friends do. And in the end, you will find that all roads lead to the same place. You and

I will go to a wonderful home I have prepared for you. But that's in the future. Until then, you have adventures to experience and wisdom to learn. Until then, you have one day after another, each one offering its own gift and its own surprise. Come on — walk with me."

As they say, the adventure of a lifetime begins with one step. Which step will you take today?

Part 4

OFF MY CASE

Sometimes there's a pretty wide gap between Sunday school lessons and real life, isn't there? On one hand, it's not hard to understand a Bible verse like 1 Peter 3:15: "Always be ready to give an answer to anyone who asks you about the hope you have." But ...

Are you ready?

Well ... maybe. But it's okay to admit that we sometimes let a chance to share our faith slip by. After all, for most of us it's hard to think of just walking up to someone and telling them how much Jesus loves them — even if we know it's true!

So that's why we're including this section of the book: some stories to help you see that everyday life is full of open doors to present the case for Christ.

You'll read four short stories of everyday kids in everyday situations. Well, mostly everyday situations. Maybe you've never worked for a family circus or lived in Mexico before. But no matter what, you'll be able to relate to the kids and the everyday jams they get themselves into.

Oh, and if any of the stories ring a bell in other ways, that's because they're built on ideas you've already learned by reading this book. In other words, these stories explain many of the cool ways to help us better understand Bible truths. Things like, can we know Jesus was real by seeing what his disciples did? These stories start with that kind of question, but then show us what might happen if kids draw pictures of the truth using their lives as pencils and paper.

Of course, they're not all perfect kids, and sometimes they mess up. But hey, everyone makes mistakes sometimes!

As you read, imagine yourself in each of the stories. That way, you'll start seeing how everyday stuff in your own life can open the door to faith in exciting new ways. Let the stories give you ideas of your own. More important, take a couple of minutes at the end of each story to answer the Go

Ahead, Stump Me! questions. Don't worry! You won't be graded, and we didn't write them to give you a hard time. But we guarantee they'll help you start thinking about how to work these ideas into your own life. After all, that's what *Case for Christ* is all about.

So have fun with the stories, and as you read them you'll discover brand-new ways to make a case for Christ. And see? It's not that hard after all!

Chapter 9

LYDIA DELGADO: MISSIONARY TO THE RICH

Lydia saw it coming, but that didn't make it hurt any less. She stepped high over Mandy Witherspoon's outstretched foot so she wouldn't trip, but she lost her grip on her books. And the kids' giggles made her face flush like fire.

"Come on, let's go!" The bus driver looked up in the rearview mirror and yelled at her. "And if you're late again tomorrow morning, you're going to have to find your own ride — or walk."

Lydia held the tears in — just barely — scooped up her books, and scrambled off the bus as fast as her legs would take her.

"Speak English much?"

She didn't turn to see who had yelled the insult, but she could guess. Mandy Witherspoon. What did that girl have against her? She wished she didn't hear some of the taunts at school, wished she understood why some of the kids looked at her with so much hatred sometimes.

"You don't belong here!"

"Get back over the border where you came from!"

But we're not going back. Lydia stood in her muddy front yard for a minute, catching her breath and letting the rain wash the tears from her face. She didn't really miss what they'd left behind in Mexico. Except back there, everybody else was just as poor as Lydia and her mother. Just as poor, and just as desperate to find something better. At least here ...

"At least here what, Lord?" she prayed out loud as she pushed open the front door to their apartment. Her thirteen-year-old sister wasn't home, as usual. And her grandmother would not return home for another two hours, maybe later, depending on what shift they gave her at the burger place. "What do we have now that's better than back home?"

Well, plenty, when she stopped to think about it. She sat down at the wobbly kitchen table and spread out her soggy books. Books, for one thing. A school to go to, and not all the kids were as mean as Mandy Witherspoon. A tiny apartment with a bathroom and a telephone. Three small rooms, which was not much compared to what a lot of other Americans had.

But compared to what they had back in Mexico? She would not soon forget the tar-paper shack they used to live in, her and a dozen other relatives: aunts and uncles and nieces and nephews, and all without a bathroom. She rested her head on her open English textbook for a minute, telling the Lord she was sorry for the way she complained. He had brought them here for a reason, she knew. She and Grandmother had prayed about it, looked for the answer.

"I'm sorry, God. Help me to know why I'm here, and what you want me to do."

But she was tired of trying to figure it out.

Right now she would close her eyes for just a minute ...

"Lydia?"

Lydia felt a soft hand on her shoulder, shaking her awake. Her grandmother stood over her, still in her fast-food uniform. Lydia didn't quite follow. She had just laid her head down a minute ago.

"What are you doing home so early?"

"Early? How long have you been sleeping? It's almost six thirty."

What? Lydia jumped up, nearly knocking over one of the bags of groceries now covering the table. She must have fallen asleep.

"And look at all this!" Her grandmother brought one last bag in from the hallway and set it down with a clunk on the kitchen table. She pointed to at least a dozen bags, now piled all over. Each one was stuffed with good things: canned peaches, a large ham, cranberries...

"I've never tasted these before." Lydia brought the can closer to see. Unreal. Everything looked so ...

"And look here!" Her grandmother pulled out a large frozen bird. "Not just one turkey...two!"

Two turkeys! It was easy to dance about the kitchen, arm in arm, giggling at each new discovery, pulling out packages of marshmallows and spaghetti, canned tuna and sweet potatoes. So many strange foods. Did all Americans eat like this? Would they?

"A feast!" her grandmother cried, but then she stopped and looked Lydia in the eye. "But tell me the truth — you didn't hear?"

"I didn't even hear you come in."

"Then who brought all this? It was all left outside the door."

Lydia had no clue, except that she'd heard church groups sometimes delivered groceries to needy families during the holidays. And they, it seemed, were one of those needy families. But when she looked at her grandmother, they both smiled at the same time. For a moment they felt more like sisters than grandmother and grand-daughter, *abuela* and *nieta*.

"Are you thinking what I'm thinking?" Lydia asked, and Grandmother nodded her head.

"I think so. We each take a bag, and come back for more."

"One bag for each house?"

That would be fine, so they pulled cans and hams from one bag to the other, spreading out the gifts they would take to others who were less fortunate than they.

God had given them this food for a reason,

had he not? And this would be part of the answer to their prayers, would it not?

Lydia couldn't keep the grin from her face as they hurried out into the cold, driving rain. Now the weather didn't matter.

"Which house first?" she asked as they hurried down the street. That would not be the hard part. The hard part was getting away from the families who discovered them before they could get away. One older woman started crying and wanted them to come into her tiny apartment.

"Thank you, no." Lydia's *abuela* smiled and held her granddaughter's hand. "We have more to deliver before it gets too late, and we're far from home. But ..."

She paused, and Lydia filled in what they had already told a handful of other families. How much they loved Jesus, and how he had answered their prayers. Each time she said it to someone new, she felt a little less shy. He had given them so much, even before the groceries; otherwise, she knew, they would not be doing this.

And for the first time, Lydia knew it was really true. The old woman looked at them with tears in her eyes.

"But we just want you to know ..." Lydia added, and it wasn't as hard to say now as it was the first time. "We want you to know how much Jesus loves you."

They left the old woman watching them through the window, and Lydia paused for a moment outside an older mobile home, looking something like the *Titanic* in its last moments. A dog growled from the darkness.

"Here?" Lydia wondered, still holding a grocery bag with their one remaining turkey. Her grandmother looked back at her with concern on her face. But Lydia didn't wait, just pushed open the gate and threaded her way past parts of a junk car as she walked up to the door. The dog went wild behind the door when she knocked.

"Anybody home?" She tried again, but no one came to the door. This would be one of the times they would just leave the bag of groceries on the front step and hope for the best. Oh, well. Lydia headed back down the walkway and almost reached the street when she heard a door squeak open. She turned around to find a girl standing in the light of the doorway, her blond hair framed in the light.

Lydia couldn't move. A streetlight flickered overhead, just bright enough to show the girl inside. So this was where Mandy Witherspoon lived. Finally Lydia backpedaled enough to leave the yard.

"Merry Christmas." Lydia forced the words from her mouth, though it wasn't quite as hard as she thought. "And ... Jesus loves you, Mandy."

BRIEFCASE

- More people than ever speak Spanish in the United States! In fact, between the years 1990 and 2000, the number of Hispanics (people whose families came from Latin America) quadrupled in places like Georgia and Tennessee. We'd better learn to say a little more than just "Hola!"

- The Hispanic church is growing quickly. Today, nine out of ten Hispanics say they're Christians. Many are Catholic, though the Spanish-speaking Protestant Church is growing too.

GO AHEAD, STUMP ME!

· How hard is it to share what you believe with people who will probably want to hear? What about with people you think may not want to hear? (Read Jonah chapter 4.)

· Imagine you are in Lydia's position. Would you share your newfound wealth? Why or why not?

· Imagine you're not as poor as Lydia. Do you share already, even if it seems like a lot? How can you share more with others?

Chapter 10
THE GREATEST SHOW IN CINCINNATI

"W hy can't you learn how to use a toilet like everyone else?"

Anthony scowled as he grabbed a snow shovel. Sure, he would clean up after her — but that didn't mean he had to like it. That didn't mean he had to like any of it, no matter how cool it might seem to someone on the outside. Nothing seemed cool when he had to clean up after a three-ton elephant every day.

Meanwhile, Penny rocked from side to side, the way elephants do, and eyed him suspiciously. Anthony's dad sometimes said that elephants could understand more than you knew.

Anthony wasn't so sure.

"Hey, kid, what's up?" An older man shuffled through the tent, his two-foot-long shoes flapping as he walked. Ricardo's eyes always looked kind of funny; he never seemed to be able to get all the clown makeup off his face.

"What's it look like?" Anthony kept shoveling. "Just the same old poop."

"Ah, so it's you against the elephant today, huh?" Ricardo stopped with his hands on his hips, like he was going to fix all of Anthony's problems. "You want to talk about it?"

Anthony just shook his head.

"Guess it wouldn't help to remind you how many other twelve-year-olds get to travel with the Bayley Brothers Family Circus, right?"

Give the clown credit. He was trying. Finally Anthony sighed and leaned against his shovel.

"I'm sorry." He wished he meant it. "Didn't

mean to be rude. But you can't tell me any other kid my age would die for a chance to do what I do."

He chuckled as he looked at the wheelbarrow full of elephant dung. Most of what Anthony did was a lot of work. Work the ring during performances. Help the moving crews. Take care of the animals. Set up the sound system. Working in his family's traveling circus was just "everyday" life.

"Sometimes I just want to be normal," he went on, and his voice dropped to a whisper. "Not moving every couple of weeks to a new city. You know, have real friends, go to a real school?"

The clown bit his lip and rubbed some of the white makeup off his cheek with his shirtsleeve.

"You ever talk to your folks about how you feel?"

Anthony shook his head again and tossed the shovel aside. What good would talking do? The Bayley family had been running this circus for three generations, and everybody knew that Anthony would be the fourth.

Had anyone ever run away *from* the circus before? He hurried from the tent, out to the Cincinnati fairgrounds where they had set up, not really knowing which direction to turn.

He slowed when he neared a group of kids his age, the kind who liked to come to the show and make a lot of noise or eat a lot of junk food. Three guys and a couple of girls stood in front of a cotton-candy stand, and the guys were probably trying their best to look impressive. Two were twirling around on their bikes, doing tricks but not very well. Anthony pretended to stoop down and tie his shoes to hear what they were talking about.

"What's the big deal with the ropewalkers, anyway?" Biker number one almost fell. Smooth move. "I think it's all fake, like, the top of the rope is flat or something. Anybody could do it."

Anthony snorted at the dumb remark. He knew better; he'd tried it a time or two himself. And there was no trick, just hours and hours of practice with ropes and harnesses and stubborn performers who wouldn't give up. But when a couple of the girls looked over at him, he covered his mouth with his hand and coughed. One of the girls smiled at him.

Anthony strolled up a little closer to the group, looking for a way to hang out without looking too obvious. Cotton candy? He fished out a couple of bucks from his pocket to buy some of the sticky treat, which gave him a chance to look like he was supposed to be there.

He hated cotton candy.

But he would stand by the group of kids

while he ate it, listening while the boys trashed each circus act.

The clowns? Lame, said the guys.

The high wire? One of the performers fell into the net, which proved they were total amateurs.

The elephants? Dumb, and one of them couldn't do the sit-up-and-beg trick.

And the tiger tamer?

"I heard they drug the animals," said the second bike-twirler, and the other expert was nodding his head. "And did you see the trainer guy? He's got to be whacked to get in there with those things."

By the way they were grinning and nodding their heads, everyone seemed to agree.

"And besides that," he went on, "he looked like he wet his pants."

They all laughed at that commentary on the Bayley Brothers' most famous act, and Anthony felt his hands go cold when he realized he was smiling along.

Smiling along? Wait a minute. What was he doing?

"They don't drug the animals." He dropped the uneaten cotton candy into the trash and wiped his hands on his back pockets. "And the tiger tamer isn't whacked — or scared."

If they hadn't noticed him before, they did now.

"Well, excuuuze me." The guy who had been doing most of the talking spread out his hands and made a face. "But who are you?"

"Anthony Bay — " He cut the last name short, and he was glad he wasn't wearing one of his bright orange Bayley Brothers Family Circus T-shirts. At least not this time. "Er, just Anthony."

"Okay, just Anthony. So they pay you to say that kind of thing?"

"I wish." Anthony shrugged.

Actually, he wished a lot of things. Wished he could say something smart. And that he'd found some other place to take a break from shoveling elephant dung.

"So what makes you the expert?" The kid on bike number one wasn't going to let this drop so easily. What else could Anthony say?

"Because ... my dad is the tiger tamer you're talking about." There. He'd said it. "And I guess I'd know if he was crazy or scared. In case you're wondering, he's not either."

Well, that pretty much did it. As the kids all stared at him Anthony backed up a couple of steps and stumbled into the trash can.

"You're not kidding, are you?" asked the girl who had first smiled at him. "So is your dad really ... Are you really ...?"

"My last name is Bayley." Anthony dug a hand into his pocket and jerked his thumb at a hanging circus sign. "Yeah, that's me."

So much for making friends. Now he was back to being part of the freak show. Only this time, he wasn't so sure it was such a horrible thing. After all, he wasn't going to change his name or anything. And something in his pocket gave him an idea. He pulled out a fistful of free passes, the kind they gave out to newspaper reporters and other VIPs. He held them out to the group.

"Maybe you want to check out the show again, now that you know it's not fake?"

Well, who would say no to free passes? Anthony smiled as he gave them each one. This time, though, nobody mentioned lame clowns or drugged animals.

"So I'll see you at the show," he told them as he turned to go. And this time he looked up at the Bayley Brothers sign...

And smiled.

BRIEFCASE

- People who lived and worked in a traveling circus used to have lots of funny customs and superstitions. For instance, many circus folks believed that peacock feathers were bad luck, while the hair from the tail of an elephant was good luck. Ever seen an elephant-hair ring or bracelet?

- The ancient Romans had a kind of circus, though it was pretty nasty, and not all performers made it out of their staged fights alive. For years, though, the circus was forgotten—unless you counted traveling jugglers or singers. Then in the late 1760s, Philip Astley in England created the modern circus, starting with riding tricks and funny acts. And the rest is history!

GO AHEAD, STUMP ME!

· Imagine how Anthony felt when he heard people making fun of his father. What did he say that made a difference?

· What would you say to someone who feels that Jesus was "off his rocker," or who just makes fun of him?

· Read some places in the Bible that defend Jesus against people who would attack him. (Check out Matthew 10:22-33.) What does Jesus promise he will do for those who speak up for him?

· Think about how Anthony explained his father to the other kids. When you know someone well, like a parent or a friend, is it easier to explain the truth about them to others? Does that same idea apply when you talk about Jesus?

Chapter 11
FAIR AND WARMER

And Josh, you're going to be working with Whitney on your weather-reporting project." Miss Peterson looked over the top of her eyeglasses at the class. "Is that all right with both of you?"

Josh shrugged and sort of grinned. "Cool."

No, no, no! Working with Josh Insley was

definitely *not* cool, not even close. But what could Whitney do about it now, besides run from the room and never come back? This is what happened when she and the class druggie were both absent from Natural Sciences class at the same time.

Of course when Miss Peterson glanced her way, Whitney had no choice except to nod and smile like a cheerleader. *Thanks so much for ruining my life, Miss Peterson.* Smiling outside, screaming inside — but that was her life.

"All right, then." As far as Miss Peterson was concerned, the matter was settled with a quick clap of her hands. "We'll continue planning the projects in groups for the rest of the period. Josh and Whitney, you'll both have some work to make up, since you're a day behind."

Whitney covered her forehead and tried to think of a way to survive this nightmare. She could do one of three things:

THING ONE: Pretend to work with Josh, sharing the failing grade he would surely earn and deserve. Well, that was an option, she supposed. Just not one she was willing to take.

THING TWO: Do all the work herself, and allow him to cruise along with her for an A. This would be the only real option that would help her protect her perfect grade point average. And if Miss Peterson found out? Well, Whitney would just tell the truth.

THING THREE: Go back home to bed and pretend she was too sick to go back to school until the earth science presentations were all over. If only ...

Actually, none of the options sounded very good. And Josh just slumped in his chair with that glazed-over look of his. Ever since the eighth grade, he and his friends had always disappeared somewhere during lunch hour. She didn't want to know where. All she knew was that if she believed something, Josh was sure to make fun of it. He would argue against anything she said, anything she believed.

This was her science partner? She didn't wait, just started scribbling notes until Josh dragged his chair over to her desk.

"All right, partner," he drawled, "what's the plan?"

Whitney held her breath and tried not to breathe the ashtray scent on his clothes. Could she get cancer from that kind of thing? She wasn't actually sure. But she knew they had to get going on this, especially since Miss Peterson was staring at them. "All right." She scribbled her plans furiously, not looking up. "I'll read the report if you run the camera. You can do that, can't you?"

"You must really think I'm pretty stupid, huh?" He lowered his voice, and the back of Whitney's neck heated up. Finally she looked at him and bit her lip.

"No, I don't think you're stupid. Let's just figure out what we should say about predicting hurricanes and get this over with."

"Predicting hurricanes," Josh said as he shrugged. "Fine."

Amazing. At least he agreed with her on that. The thing was, he didn't turn out to be as dense as she had feared. In fact, as they dived into their research, she realized he knew the Internet much better than she did, probably because of all the raunchy sites probably he visited. But Whitney didn't dare say anything about that.

"So you want to say something about this in the report?" he asked her as he drilled through some notes on how weather experts knew how to guess where hurricanes would go. The notes would become part of what Whitney was going to read on camera, as if she were a weather expert explaining the next hurricane. Like on TV.

"Sure, uh ..." She did her best to keep up with what he was typing. At least they would be able to catch up to the rest of the class, no problem. But just because Josh was a little sharper than she'd expected, well, that didn't change his attitude. He looked up at her with a raised eyebrow.

"You going to try to slip in anything about how God makes the weather?"

Where had that come from? She snapped her mouth shut, trying to figure out how to defend herself.

"I don't know," she finally admitted. "Although maybe it's not such a bad thought."

"Hey, whoa." He put up his hands. "I wasn't trying to give you any ideas."

"You brought it up, not me."

Half an hour later he would bring it up again. Only this time they were out in back of the auditorium, where Josh had the school video camera trained on her, and she was getting ready to read their script about predicting hurricanes. Kind of reminded her of the youth group video scavenger hunt they were planning at church, only this time she had to hold on to her hair to keep from being blown away. And this time she was rethinking their idea to do this outside.

"So if your God knows all about the weather," Josh asked her as he looked up at a dark cloud, "how come he doesn't give us a better clue, sometimes?"

She noticed the camera's red light blinking at her. The tape was rolling? Was he trying to make her look foolish?

"We just have to know where to look, I guess."

"Yeah, right. Sounds pretty convenient." He adjusted the camera on its stand as she spoke. "You pray, and God tells you the future, a hundred percent. Just like he tells you the winning lottery ticket numbers."

"Maybe not the lottery ticket numbers." Whitney knew where she was taking this, now. After all, she might never have a chance to talk to this boy again — or want to — on camera or off. "But sometimes he does tell the future."

"No kidding? Now that I'd like to see."

"Then all you have to do is check out the Old Testament."

"I knew it! You mean like the secret Bible code."

"No, no. Nothing bogus like that. Just dozens of predictions about how Jesus would come. Actually, I don't know how many, but there were a whole lot."

"Like about what?"

"Like what he would be like. What he would do. Even how he would die."

"I heard once that there was a guy named Nostradamus who did some of that kind of thing. Told the future."

"No, no. Not like Nostradamus. This was all

written in the Old Testament, hundreds of years before it happened. And every prediction was one hundred percent on. So it wasn't like a fortune-teller ... or a hurricane prediction."

"Hmm. A hundred percent?" Josh scratched the peach-fuzz goatee on his chin, like he didn't believe a word she was saying. At least this time he didn't have a snappy comeback, so maybe he was thinking about it.

And still the camera blinked, so she figured she'd better pick up her script and start talking about how to predict hurricanes. But that's when a gust of wind lifted up a trash bucket and sent it scuttling their way.

"Whitney!" Josh yelled at her. "Watch it!"

This was no hurricane, but —

"Keep the camera rolling," she ordered, just as the sky opened up and dumped a thunderstorm full of rain on their heads, just as the trash bucket bumped by behind her. Josh got the idea and grinned as she recited the introduction to their report.

"Is the next hurricane going to be a level one, a level two, or even stronger?" She cupped a hand over her face to shield the rain, now pouring and matting down her hair. But this time she didn't care. "It's hard to tell, and scientists don't always know ..."

A gust of wind nearly ripped the script from her hand, but she kept going.

"Unless they know how to look for the right clues."

BRIEFCASE

- The great Galveston hurricane hit coastal Texas on September 8, 1900. Most people in Galveston had no warning that their city was about to be leveled and that more than 8,000 people would die. Imagine trying to predict hurricanes before satellite photos and storm-tracker planes!

- It's hard to say how many places in the Old Testament point to the coming of a Savior. But there are hundreds, starting in Genesis and going straight through to Malachi. Check out especially Psalm 22 and Isaiah 53. In the passage in Psalms, for instance, you'll find eleven places that mention details of how Jesus would die. And that was written a thousand years before it happened!

GO AHEAD, STUMP ME!

· How do you think all those prophets knew that Jesus was coming? Do you think it was coincidence?

· What would you say to someone who might think all the prophecies were written AFTER Jesus was born?

· How do you treat someone who dresses or acts differently from you? Are you afraid to talk to them? If not, how do you feel?

Chapter 12

I SAW ELVIS!

L ord, we want to be good examples for you, but …" Nate kept his head bowed as he and Aaron prayed in the back room behind the stage. No one would see the two friends there, for now. The only thing was, Nate couldn't keep his hands — or his voice — from shaking.

"But when everybody in the audience is going to be staring at us," Aaron said, picking up the prayer, "it's pretty tough."

No kidding. Nate wasn't sure he liked being reminded, but it was true. Every mom, dad, and grandparent was sitting out in the Franklin Middle School auditorium, waiting for the annual talent show to start. Plus their youth pastor, Bill Stewart, and a bunch of people from church. Not to mention a photographer from the Franklin *News-Dispatch*, who was probably there to take a picture of the $250 first-prize winner.

Was it too late to slip out of the building, maybe hide in Aaron's basement?

"So please help us not to croak in front of everyone." Nate finished up the tag-team prayer. "In Jesus' name — "

Almost. The storage room door burst open before he got to the "amen," and a guy with long painted-on black sideburns and a glittery white suit poked his head inside.

"Whoa!" Elvis stepped back for a moment, then grinned like a fisherman with a big fish on the line. "A-MEN, brothers! I be-LEEVE!"

Too bad you don't really, thought Nate. Not that they hadn't tried inviting him to youth group for the past umpteen years. At first they'd thought he might be interested, since his grandpa had been some kind of famous preacher. But all they'd ever heard back were the usual dumb lines, like "Yeah, I'll come, maybe next year."

Well, next year came and went, and Jeremy was a tough case, all right. Smart — and he knew all the Christian lingo. The weird part was, he could curse like a sailor one minute and tell a crazy joke the next. And now he blocked the door, wearing that teasing grin of his that sent a chill up Nate's spine.

"Except praying isn't going to help you much," he told them. "Not when you're up against the King."

"Ha!" Aaron blurted out. "All you're doing is imitating some singer guy who died years ago. What's so cool about that?"

"Aaron." Nate elbowed his best friend. Aaron was pretty good at saying whatever came to his mind, usually before he thought it through. But it was too late. Jeremy had already taken the challenge, and his dark eyes narrowed when he looked at them.

"And all you're doing is praying to some religious dude who got himself killed two thousand years ago, and all his buddies besides. Tell me, what's the difference?"

Whoa. Nate shivered like they'd just been hit by a blast from a quick-freezer. And no, they hadn't seen this side of Jeremy before. Not quite. Aaron choked on his spit.

"Hey, relax, man." The easy grin crept back on Jeremy's face. "If it works for you, no problem. Make you feel better? I just came to say that I hope you weren't planning on winning the show, 'cause — "

"We'll make you a deal," Aaron interrupted. "If we finish ahead of you, all you have to do is come to our youth group party afterward."

Dude. Nate was ready to slide off his chair, because his best friend had a death wish. But Jeremy only seemed to think a moment before he grinned and held out his hand.

"Deal. And if I finish ahead of you ..." He paused. "You promise to stop laying all the Jesus stuff on me. Forever. I already heard it all from my grandpa."

Aaron looked him straight in the eye and shook the other boy's hand. Only with the costume and all it looked like he was shaking Elvis's hand, which was kind of comical, so Nate did his best not to think of it that way. Jeremy scowled at him.

"Something funny?"

"No, no." Nate zipped his lip and shook his head. "We probably need to get ready, though."

"Ten minutes, Brother Nathan." The Elvis impersonator straightened his swoopy-haired black wig. "Break a leg."

Weird. Nate wasn't sure what made him shake more — their strange bargain with Jeremy Winston, or the talent show itself.

"We'll be there." Aaron made for the door.

"I'll tell Mrs. Mac you're going to open the show in prayer," Jeremy joked.

Knowing Jeremy Winston, he just might.

"How about if I pull his microphone plug in the middle of his act?" Nate mumbled as he clenched his fist and followed Jeremy to where everyone was gathering behind the stage.

"Oh ye of little faith." Aaron looked all business. "We're going to win. And we still have to be a witness."

"A witness, yes," Nate whispered back. "Not a joke."

Nobody said their two-man juggling act was going to be serious. At least their show was pretty good, since they had been practicing for the past couple of months in Nate's garage. So when it was their turn they dropped the bowling pins only once, and people clapped at the end of the act.

"Pretty good, huh?" Nate said it only loud enough for Aaron to hear, and they bowed once more before they left the stage. Everybody slapped them on the back or gave them a high five. Even Jeremy.

"Not bad." Jeremy adjusted his costume once more. He was up next. "Maybe you'll get second or third."

Well, it didn't take long to figure out they weren't placing first. Nate had to admit it: Jeremy was good. Awfully good. When it was his turn, he did the Elvis shimmy, the Elvis slouch, the Elvis voice. He even grabbed the microphone and twisted it around like Elvis. A bunch of girls in the front row screamed for fun. And after Jeremy finished telling everybody they weren't nothing but a hound dog, the audience even gave him a standing ovation.

"Thank you." Jeremy smiled out at the crowd in excellent Elvis form. "Thank you very much."

Nate even caught himself smiling and clapping with the rest of them. Whoops.

"Hey!" Aaron punched him in the arm. "Whose side are you on?"

"Sorry." Nate shrugged. "He was good."

The problem was, Jeremy knew it too.

"No hard feelings, huh?" Jeremy met them as

he strutted off the stage. "The King was just too good for the Bible Boys, I guess."

Nate could imagine the steam pouring out of Aaron's ears. But he forced himself to shake Jeremy's hand.

"You did a good job playing a dead guy," Nate told him.

"Don't you read those newspapers they sell in the supermarket checkout lines?" Jeremy laughed. "People have seen Elvis alive, like in a Seven-Eleven in Arizona."

"Okay." Nate played along. "But what if Mrs. Mac said she'd flunk you unless you admitted the truth — that Elvis was dead?"

Jeremy stopped rubbing at the stage make-up on his face long enough to give them a curious look. He'd won his bet, but there really weren't any other ways to answer the question.

"Seriously." Nate pressed his point, since they might not get another chance. "What would you say then?"

"If I was going to flunk? What do you think? It's just a joke, okay? Nobody's going to take a hit for something they don't really believe."

"Bingo." Nate snapped his fingers. "So don't you think all the disciples were telling the truth about Jesus — especially when they got killed for it?"

The Bible Boys left Jeremy standing back-stage in his Elvis costume, holding his wig and looking more confused than they'd ever seen him.

"You're still welcome to come to youth group," Aaron added with a smile. "Except, whoops! Sorry. We're not supposed to mention it to you anymore."

Somehow Nate figured it didn't matter, this time. And he had a feeling Jeremy might finally show up.

BRIEFCASE

• Elvis Presley was born in a small house in Tupelo, Mississippi, in 1935, and became a superstar singer by combining pop, country, gospel, and R&B styles. Though he died in 1977, more than a billion copies of his records have been sold, which is more than any other performer. Despite silly stories printed occasionally in supermarket tabloids, he is not still alive.

• According to early church historians, all of Jesus' disciples were killed for what they believed and preached except John. Matthew died of sword wounds in Ethiopia. Mark was dragged through the streets of Alexandria, Egypt, behind a chariot. Luke was hanged in Greece. And the list goes on ...

GO AHEAD, STUMP ME!

· Imagine you were a friend of Lazarus when he died.
You're sad – but then he walks back into the room! What
do you think about that? (Read the story in John
chapter 11 of your Bible.)

· What would you say if someone asked you, "Come on,
now. A dead man can't really come back, can he?"

· Do you think Jesus was really dead in the first place?
And if you do, why do you think Jesus came back?

· Imagine you were one of the first disciples. Would you
have died for something you didn't believe in – or that
you knew wasn't true? What does history tell you
about what the disciples believed?

We want to hear from you. Please send your comments about this book to us in care of zreview@zondervan.com. Thank you.